From Award-Winning Author

LITERARY TITAN BOOK AWARD

Sacred Geometry for Healing

MANTRAS AND MANDALAS FOR MEDITATION

Adria Chalfin

Copyright © 2025

Adria Chalfin

All rights reserved.

ISBN: 9780997847833

Mantras and Mandalas Guide for Meditations

Each mandala in this book has a universal and personal meaning. Each title and aura blue print image embodies the spirit of what has been experienced in the collective consciousness of human experience, connecting to the divine. As God experiences, we experience. Choose your mandala for the moment by either concentrating and opening the book and finding your spirit guided selection or browse the titles and choose what resonates with your heart at the moment. Remember you are not alone, what you are facing and experiencing from joy to despair has been faced by those who came before you and by those that are here with you now. Focus your meditation on your selected mandala and read the corresponding mantra. You can repeat it out loud during your meditation or remain silent.

Contents
Mandalas by Title

1-Aura, 2-Golden, 3-Nature, 4-Regal, 5-Jesus Christ, 6-Crown of Thorns, 7-Crucifixion, 8-Holy Light, 9-Holy Spirit, 10-Wounded, 11-Despair, 12-The Underworld, 13-Transformation, 14-Soul, 15-Death, 16-Incarnation, 17-Defenses, 18-Tree of Life, 19-History, 20-Tribal, 21-Primitive, 22-Exertion, 23-Evolution, 24-Symbolic, 25-Cohesion, 26-Seeding, 27-Polarity, 28-Symbiotic, 29-Strength, 30-Staff of Life, 31-Feathers, 32-Rosettes, 33-Abundance, 34-Basket, 35-Energized. 36-Confusion, 37-Memories, 38-Hope, 39-Numerology, 40-Partnership, 41-Physical, 42-Heaven, 43-Ultimate, 44-Tranquility, 45-Babies, 46-Nurture, 47-Love, 48-Magic, 49-Sun, 50-Wheel of Time, 51-Angel

Mantras and Mandalas

1 'Aura'

I am clearing and cleansing my aura.
I am protecting my aura.

2

'Golden'

I am golden, I am well, I am satisfied.

3 'Nature'

My true nature is one with nature. I am natural. I am my authentic self.

4

'Regal'

I am of the divine. I stand tall. I am proud to be.

5

'Jesus Christ'

Almighty-all knowing soul, thank you for existing, for creation, for my life.

6

'Crown of Thorns'

I feel pierced as you. I feel condemned as you. May you rise and your pain be lifted. May I rise from my crucifixion. We are all one with you.

7 'Crucifixion'

Thank you for your sacrifice. I am full of sorrow. I wish for you to be free and happy now. I wish to be free and happy with you.

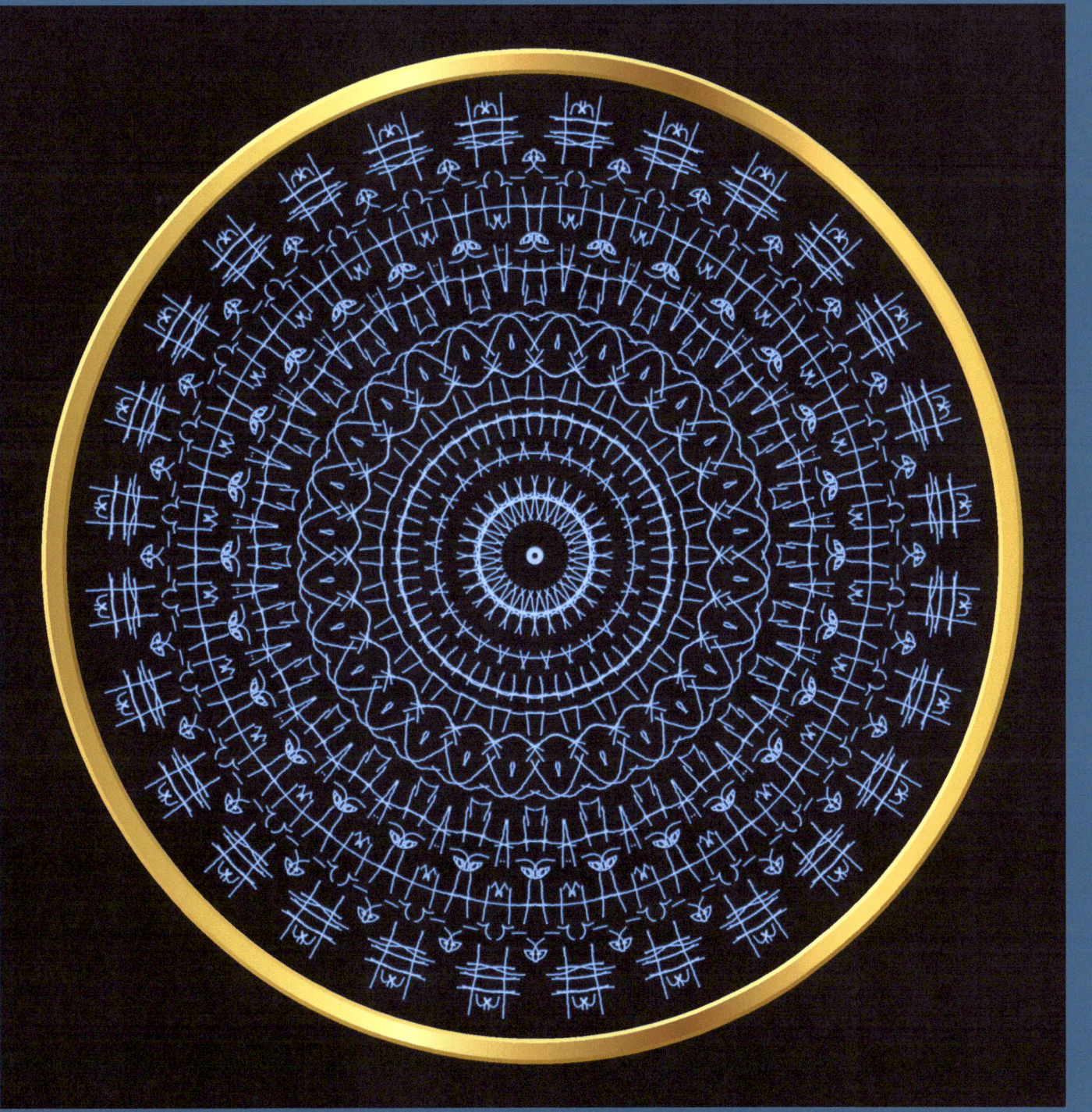

8

'Holy Light'

Oh Holy Light—I focus on you and wipe away the darkness that plagues me. Oh Holy Light in all your beauty.

9

'Holy Spirit'

I listen for you carefully—to guide me.

10 'Wounded'

Every day I am wounded. I remember I am not alone. Every day we are all wounded. I have the strength to heal and pull through.

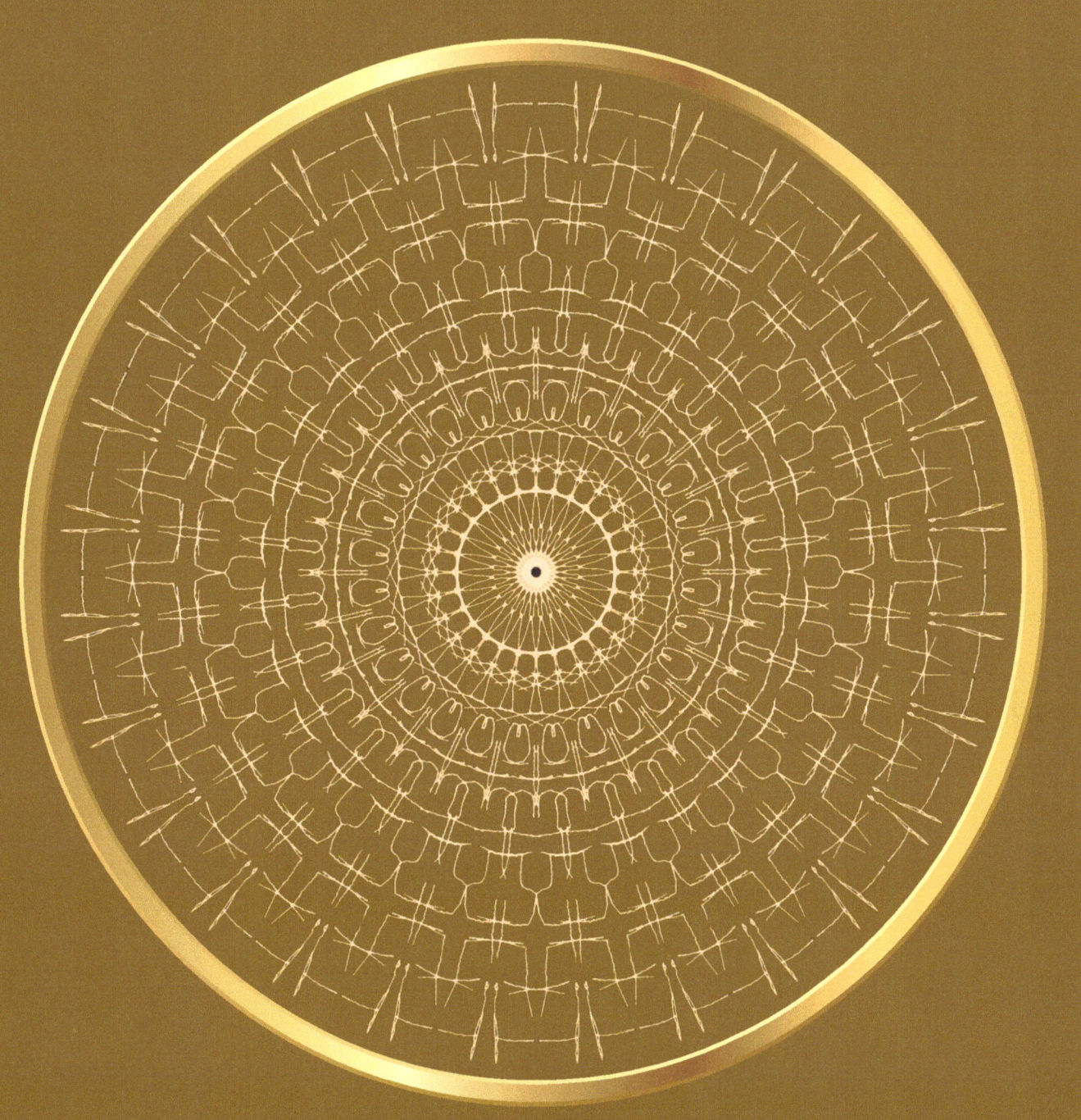

11 'Despair'

I am in despair. I am desperate. I will remember I am not alone. As every soul that has gone through this before me—I will triumph, I will make it through.

12

'The Underworld'

Creeping darkness leaking from the shadow world— be gone! I am enveloped in protection and light.

13 'Transformation'

Every day I am changing. My life is my transformation. I will trust the process.

14 'Soul'

Oh my eternal soul, you are weary. I quietly meditate to give you a moment of rest.

15 'Death'

Death, you are my fear, my anxiety, my ruin. I pray during this meditation for the new age—the end of death and dying.

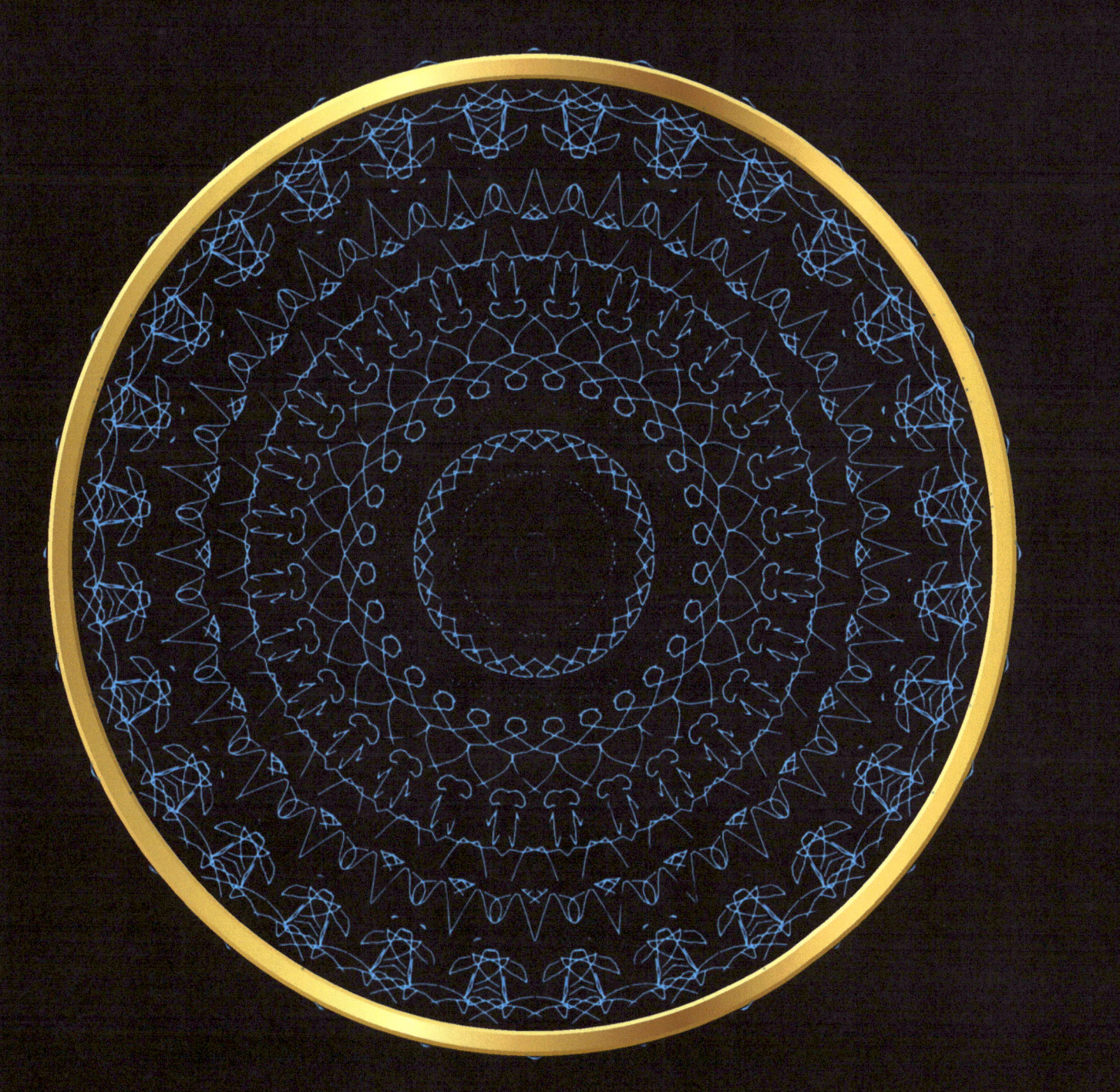

16 'Incarnation'

I am incarnate. I breathe and care for my physicality and the physical world around me. I value my body and soul equally.

17 'Defenses'

My defenses are strong.
My defenses are good.
When I feel defenseless
— I will grow more
strength with everything
I face.

18 'Tree of Life'

I am a leaf. I am a branch. I am a fruit. I am a part of the whole of creation—of The Tree of Life.

19 'History'

Akashic records that hold all the tales from all times — I admit you, that I may not invoke the repetition of history—but wish instead to bring a new way.

20 'Tribal'

My origin, my tribe—I call to you. For we have been scattered facing our own alienation. May we come together again.

21 'Primitive'

I am as my ancestors. I am origin. I am not ashamed to be my true self.

22 'Exertion'

I am overworked. I am drained too far. I remind myself that all is already perfect and I breathe and take a moment to renew.

23 'Evolution'

As I evolve, I may leave many behind. This is a natural process, I aknowledge and accept.

24 'Symbolic'

I am a symbol. My existence is symbolic of all existence. I will mindfully live my best self to represent to all—the existence that forged me.

25

'Cohesion'

I unite and I am united with all humanity, nature and creation. Here I find peace.

26 'Seeding'

Every day I plant the seeds I wish to grow—alongside all's planting in the garden of life, at the same time. May we all grow a beautiful garden—void of weeds and desolation.

27 'Polarity'

As I face opposition, as I experience ups and downs—I realign and rebalance myself in this meditation.

28 'Symbiotic'

We are all in motion at the same time. May I resonate in harmony and may my fellow occupants of life resonate in harmony with me as well.

29 'Strength'

I am weakened. I am crushed. I am exhausted. Give me strength and let me strengthen now to endure.

30

'Staff of Life'

I nourish my body with whole grain bread. I nourish my soul with self reflection, mindfulness and meditation.

31 'Feathers'

I take flight. I soar above my worldly cares and stressors. I revel here calmly for the moment.

32 'Rosettes'

I am tranquil. I am still. I radiate with beauty as a lovely rose.

33. 'Abundance'

My time of lacking has come to an end. I am filled with abundance for my body and my soul.

34 'Basket'

I am a strand of reed being woven in and out— and sometimes unraveled and redone altogether. I trust in the process of my perfect development.

35. 'Energized'

I am drained. I am depleted. I am receiving energy. I am replenishing.

36 'Confusion'

I am full of loud noise. I am confused. I cannot hear my truth. I calm myself until my path is clear.

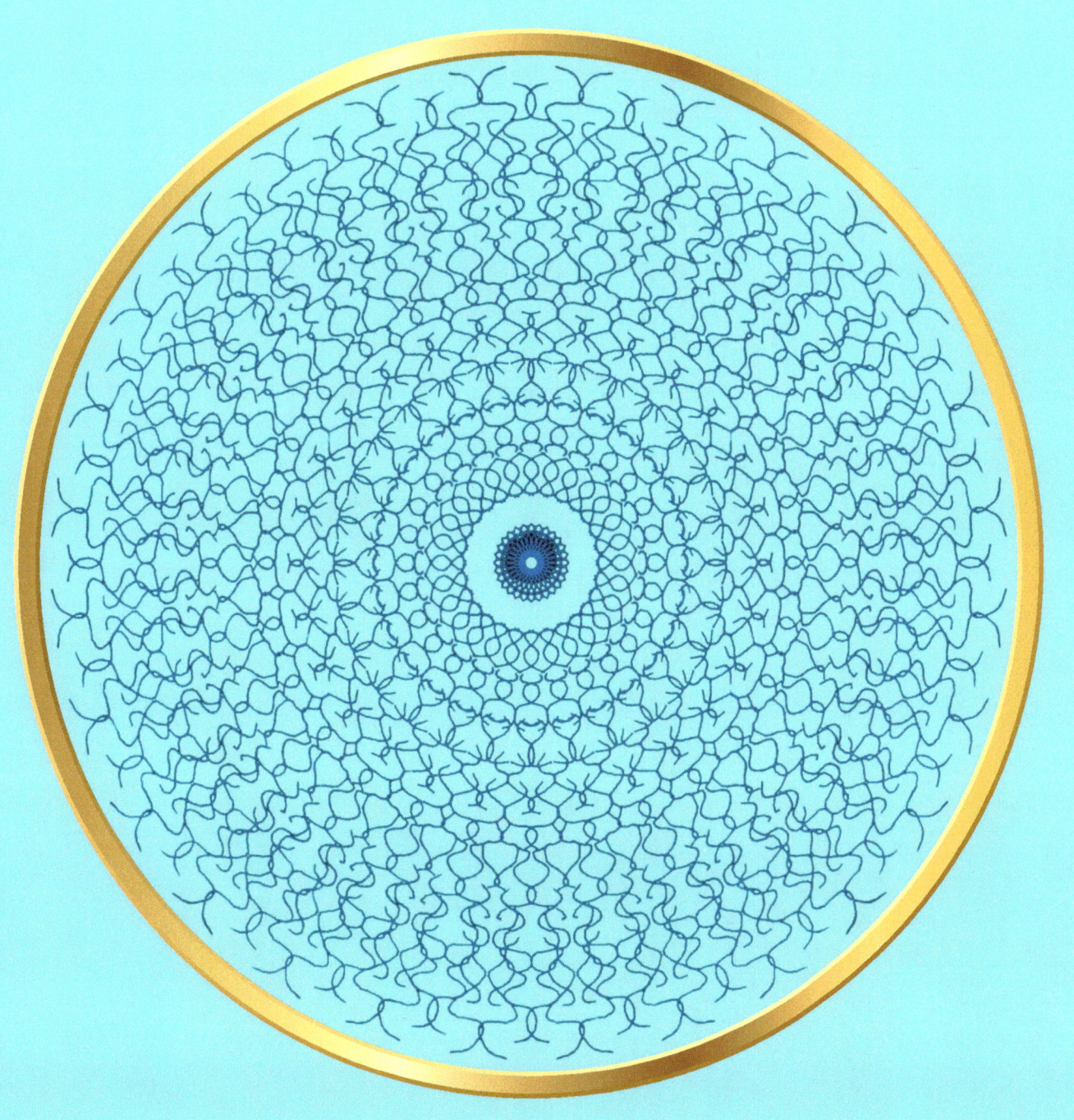

37 'Memories'

From all our past lives our traumatic memories are stored and easily triggered by a recent event.

I am stable. I am calming and healing from my karmic PTSD.

38 'Hope'

I hope for ....
I hope that ....
(Fill in the blank for the meditation and think or speak it.)

39 'Numerology'

Each number has a corresponding power, influence and meaning. I focus on the number that is in my head during my meditation.

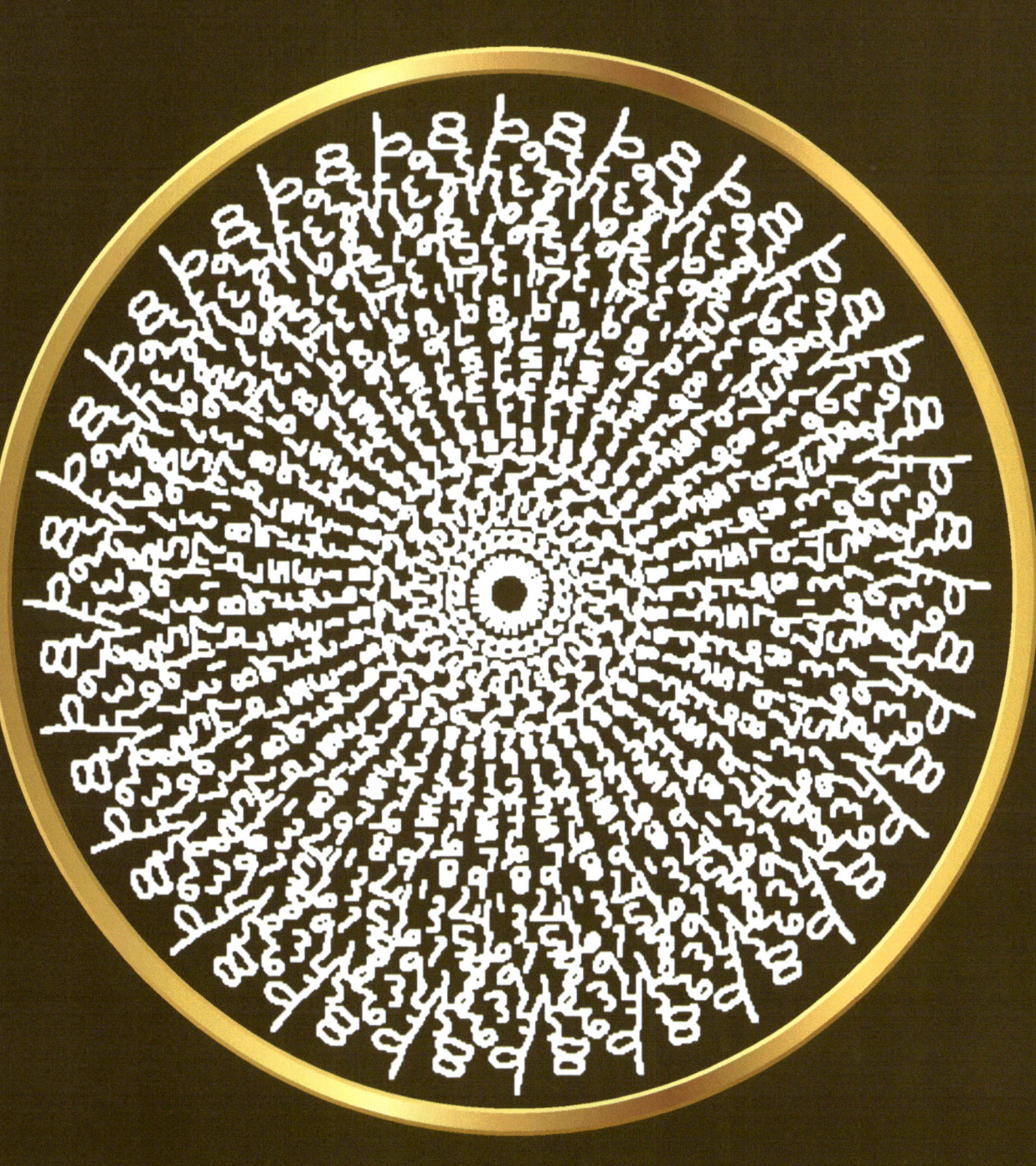

40 'Partnership'

My relationship with myself and with others is balanced, harmonious and positive. I remove the negative and destructive from my life.

41 'Physical'

On this physical plane which I reside—I manifest good and solid wishes for myself and for all.

42

'Heaven'

I focus on perfection, on the highest attainment, on a heavenly state.

43 'Ultimate'

I feel every moment to the fullest. I appreciate every moment to the fullest.

44

'Tranquility'

I am tranquil. I am calm. All thoughts, fears and anxieties have left me.

45

'Babies'

I know the joy of the cycle of life.

46

'Nurture'

I am mother.
I am father.
I am nurturer.

47

'Love'

I give, I receive, and I am complete.

48

'Magic'

Oh the mysterious, oh the magical, is not always as it seems. May the unseen magic forces be solely good and supportive.

49 'Sun'

Oh almighty Sun—thank you for your light, your warmth and your sustaining of all life.

50 'Wheel of Time'

Everlasting Time—I bow to your omnipotence, your might, your magnificence.

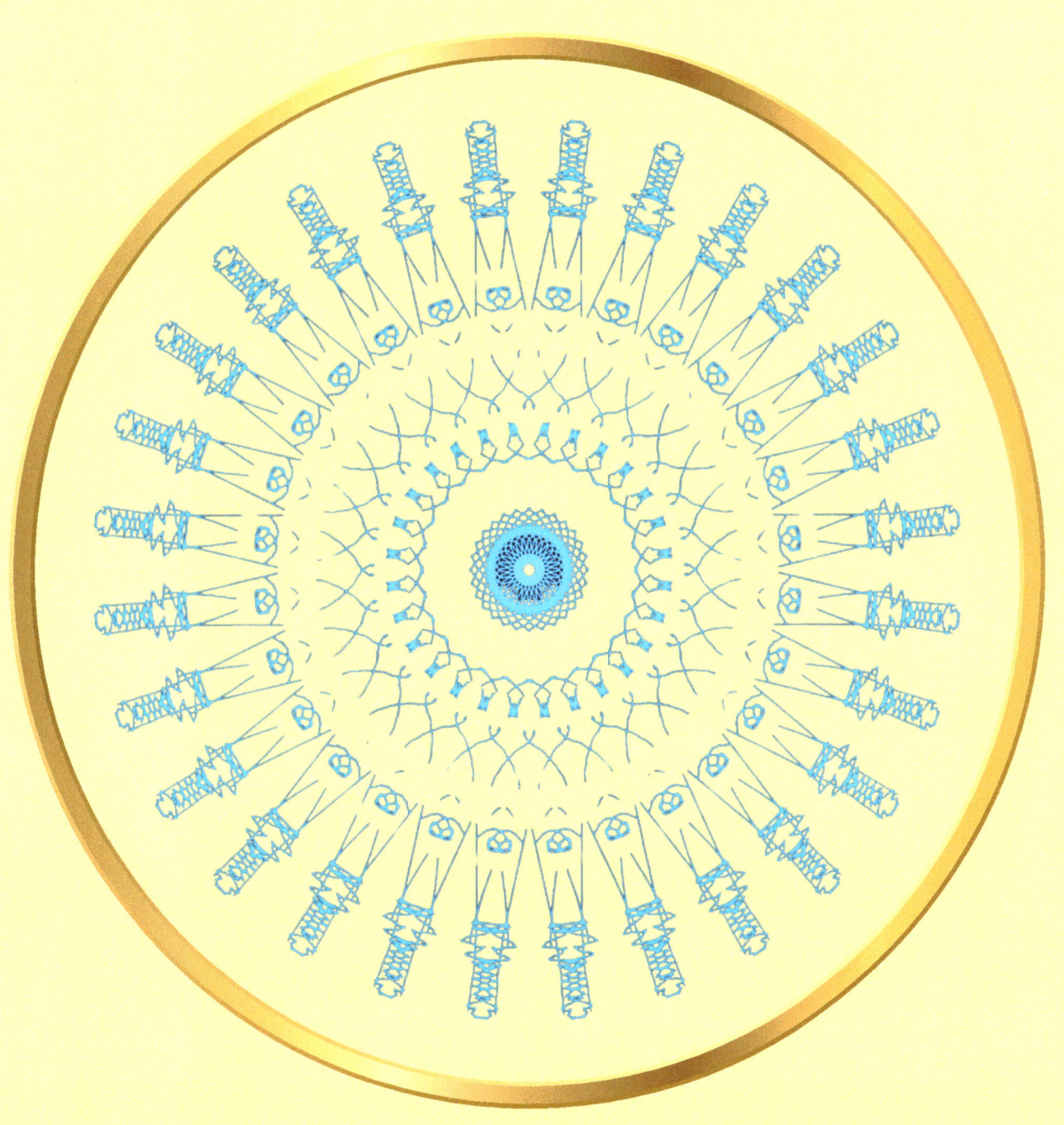

51

'Angel'

Oh heavenly Angel
Oh Angel guide
Hello!

I hope you enjoyed this book of my original art inspired
by sacred geometry, beauty and deeper meanings. It is my wish to help bring healing to our lives as a human collective and individual through meditation, mantras and mandalas.

Adria - The Artist

adriabooks.com

PO BOX 602
Los Alamos CA
93440

www.ingramcontent.com/pod-product-compliance
Lightning Source LLC
Chambersburg PA
CBHW041112070526
44584CB00002B/142